T0156386

# THE
# CONTRACTOR'S
## HOME PURCHASE
## GUIDE

## TIMOTHY PERRY
### AND
## DANIEL PROUTY

iUNIVERSE, INC.
BLOOMINGTON

# The Contractor's Home Purchase Guide

iUniverse books may be ordered through booksellers or by contacting:

iUniverse
1663 Liberty Drive
Bloomington, IN 47403
www.iuniverse.com
1-800-Authors (1-800-288-4677)

ISBN: 978-1-4620-2001-0 (sc)
ISBN: 978-1-4620-2002-7 (hc)
ISBN: 978-1-4620-2003-4 (e)

Library of Congress Control Number: 2011907619

Printed in the United States of America

iUniverse rev. date: 5/26/2011

# CONTENTS

# Introduction

**Fact: All pre-owned homes are in need of repair, remodel, or general upgrades regardless of a buyer's or seller's market.**

*The Contractor's Home Purchase Guide* was conceived between two guys who have been best friends for over fifty years and who are both passionate about construction and helping people. Timothy Perry, a current and active general contractor with more than thirty-five years of experience, is always disheartened and amazed at how home buyers are continually taken advantage of due to their overall lack of basic construction knowledge. Countless times, he has heard from disheartened home buyers, "If I only knew at the time to ask if building permits were available for the remodel" or "If I would have asked and really checked the bathroom floor, I would have seen that there was dry rot."

Tim would tell Dan about all of the various jobs he was working on—which were, for the most part, sad stories—and this compelled the two of them to provide a helpful, simple, and easy solution to assist potential home buyers. Thus the book *The Contractor's Home Buying Guide* was created. Tim provided over thirty-five years of on-site knowledge and expertise for this book, and Daniel Prouty provided the structure and format and made it happen. Dan is a financial professional who spent his early years in the retail building supply business. He also consults for Tim on his construction business.

When you buy a home, it comes packaged with hidden defects. As delighted as you may be about your new home, the defects are there, and they will cause you grief in the years to come. Will the roof need to be replaced? Is there asbestos or lead present anywhere? Is the plumbing leaking? Is the electrical capacity adequate for your needs? How much will it cost to put in a new hardwood floor or to retile a bathroom? Is the house safe against floods, fires, hurricanes, tornadoes, lightning, and earthquakes? These are serious questions. Facing up to the answers if you are not prepared will leave a sudden, unexpected void in your bank account.

These questions should be addressed before you write what is likely the biggest check of your life.

Being an aware and forewarned home buyer isn't always easy. Let's face it: in reality, enthusiasm over the house's charm and finer aesthetic attributes takes precedence over the need to study a water stain on the ceiling or descend into the basement and check for seismic anchor bolts. However, these precautions—and many others—are absolutely essential to smart home buying. Homes are extremely expensive, and so are repairs and remodels. You truly owe it to yourself to become as knowledgeable as possible regarding the condition of your prospective investment.

You, your family, and your future financial well-being are counting on it.

That's what *The Contractor's Home Purchase Guide* is all about.

This book is not about interest rates, creative financing, home owner's insurance, or how to qualify for a mortgage. This book is about having the tools, guidelines, and information required to make a sound, informed financial investment based on the current structural, code-compliant, cosmetic, and day-to-day living conditions of your prospective new home.

## YOU BE THE JUDGE

This book empowers you with the information you need to quickly spot a home's potential defects and to easily estimate on the spot the costs of repairs and replacements. In today's market of home buying, selling, and price up-bidding, *every area in need of repair, replacement, or remodeling is a negotiating or contingency point.* You don't need extensive knowledge of construction or building codes to use this simple walk-through guidebook. This book has all of the areas to address and will help you get a fair, equitable deal. It was written with the belief that you can and should be the judge of what condition your future home (investment) is in.

With this book, you are empowered! You will walk through your potential new home as if your contractor were by your side looking out for your best interest, inspecting and evaluating every potential problem area. You will see to it that your next home is a sound financial investment. If a neglected home has simply been spruced up with a little paint and new carpets, you will have the tools and ability to spot cosmetics patches as long as you have *The Contractor's Home Purchase Guide* at your side when you go house hunting so that you can buy right.

Keep this booklet in hand as you walk through your potential future home. Be sure to answer each question as you tour the various parts of the property and use the estimated dollar amounts to figure out the repair and replacement costs of each specific area from the front to the back throughout the interior. Along the way, you will be alerted to real and potential problems, along with being informed as to the cost of repairs.

When the walk-through is done, you can easily calculate the total estimated repair cost for the house. You will be able to make an informed decision about whether to go ahead with the offer to purchase. *You be the judge of whether the price is right.* If you feel it's too high, you can use what you have learned to negotiate a fair, realistic price or simply move on to the next house.

## ASSUMPTIONS

All estimates for replacement and repair include both materials and labor and are based on an 1,800-square-foot home with a two-car garage, three bedrooms, two baths, and a front and backyard.

The estimates represent an average based on the largest metropolitan cities in the United States. They are intended only as a best guesstimate guide for repair, replacement, or remodeling calculation purposes.

# How to Use This Book

You begin the evaluation of a house by answering the yes-or-no questions included in the chapters. The questions are written in such a way that *an answer of yes always indicates a problem*—or at least a potential problem. An affirmative answer thus amounts to a red flag. This makes reviewing your work fast and easy.

After the walk-through is over, compile a list of the house's potential problems together with estimated costs of repairs or replacement. Then all you do is just tally up the totals. (A worksheet for three home comparisons is included in the back of the book to make the process simple, easy, and effective.) Now you will know what the house will really cost you and whether you feel comfortable putting in an offer.

Enjoy, save, and negotiate with confidence in your search for your new, fairly priced home.

Happy house hunting!

## Things to Know Before You Go

- Do you have access to an appraisal (estimated value of the home)? Appraisals can be costly and are normally done by a licensed professional appraiser. If a current one is available, it could be useful in your ultimate decision.
- The two most important documents to have are a recent appraisal and a current, legitimate termite and pest report. You should request a copy of a current termite report (which is factual) for the houses you are looking at. Sellers are responsible for providing a termite report. Note: If you need help understanding what these reports mean, a licensed contractor can help. If the termite report is older than six months, you should ask if there is a more current one.
- Be aware of how old the homes are you are looking at.
- Know the construction dates of any remodels or modifications.
- Ask to see any building permits for remodels or modifications.

- Lead-based paints were used in most construction prior to 1978. Check the Internet or your local listings for lead-based paint removal services.
- Do you have a real estate agent/broker?
- Have you—or has your realtor—performed comparisons for comparable houses?
- Be aware that home buying can be competitive. Can you afford to get caught in a bidding war and still have enough reserve to make legitimate repairs, upgrades, and replacements?
- Have you been preapproved for a loan?
- Have you investigated the amenities, services, and personality of the neighborhood?
- Check with your local police department regarding incidents of crime in the areas in which you are looking.
- Have you explored the financing options?
- Have you explored whether alternative financing is available?
- Have you researched all city and county taxes for the areas you are interested in (schools, sewer, special assessments, etc.)?
- Home inspectors charge approximately $400 for a summary of the condition of a home.
- Sellers are not responsible for providing home inspection reports.
- Be aware of any lead or asbestos issues in any of the homes at which you are looking.

# Notes Before You Go

# The Front of the House

We begin our walk-through by taking a good, objective look at the front of the house. Though the front may look great to a casual onlooker, a closer inspection could reveal serious and costly problems. You need to address the following points:

## First Impression

_____

_____

_____

_____

_____

_____

_____

_____

_____

_____

_____

# Landscaping

**YES / NO**

_____Is sprinkler system nonfunctional?
_____Is the water pressure on the faucets too low?
_____Is the landscaping unattractive or poorly maintained?
_____Are there any trees, shrubs, or bushes that need to be removed?

# Driveway

**YES / NO**

_____Is the driveway sloped toward the house? During the rainy season, this may lead to flooding in the garage and elsewhere.
_____Are there excessive cracks in the driveway?
*Replacement cost: $12,000–$18,000 based on a 400-square-foot driveway*

# Front Walkway

**YES / NO**

_____Is the walkway leading to the front door cracked or upturned?
*Replacement cost on concrete walkway: $8 per square foot*

# Destructive Root Systems

**YES / NO**

_____Do portions of the front walkway appear uplifted and/or higher than the original position? This is most likely the work of powerful roots. In addition to causing sidewalk and driveway problems, destructive root systems sometimes wreak havoc on water and sewage lines. Perhaps the offending trees must at some point be removed, which could cost a lot of money and have a major impact on the house's appearance.

# Stairs and Landings

## Wooden

**YES / NO**

\_\_\_\_\_Do the stairs sag?

\_\_\_\_\_Are the stairs faded, cracked, or rotted?

\_\_\_\_\_Are the support posts for the stairs in contact with the ground? Contact between wood and soil leads to rot.

\_\_\_\_\_Are the handrails missing?

*Replacement cost for a one-story set of wooden stairs (thirteen steps, landing, and handrails): $1,500–$2,500*

# Concrete or Brick

**YES / NO**

\_\_\_\_\_Are the stairs or landing physically unconnected from the house itself?

\_\_\_\_\_Has the bottom stair sunk below the level of the front walkway? If so, the stairs and landing are probably sinking under their own weight.

*Replacement cost for stairs, landing, and handrail (concrete or brick): $2,500*

# Porch and Overhang

**YES / NO**

\_\_\_\_\_Does the porch's overhang (roof) appear to sag?

\_\_\_\_\_Are the supporting posts for the porch rotted? Always check where wood (posts, etc.) makes contact with soil.

*Repair cost: $500*

*Replacement cost: $1,800*

# Siding

**Wood**

**YES / NO**

_____Is there foliage against the building? If so, pull the foliage away from the building and inspect for moisture and evidence of rot.

_____In general, is the siding rotted, warped, or weathered looking? If so, replacement may be called for.

*Replacement cost: Varies depending on type of siding—get an estimate.*

# Stucco

**YES / NO**

_____Is the stucco cracked, patched, or a different color?

*Note: Check especially around windows and doorways.*

_____Is the stucco crumbling at ground level?

*Replacement cost: $5 per square foot*

# Brick and Cinder Block

**YES / NO**

_____Is there excessive paint buildup or cracking around the foundation, doorways, or windows?

*Repair cost: varies—get an estimate*

# Paint or Stain

**YES / NO**

_____Is the exterior paint or stain weathered in appearance?

*Cost to repaint exterior of house: $ 3,500–$7,500 depending on the number of colors and detail*

*Note: Older (1978 and prior) homes may contain lead-based paint.* Lead was used in oil-based paints. Latex water-based paints generally do not contain lead. The majority of the homes built between 1940 and 1978 contain leaded paint. It could be on any interior or exterior surface; pay close attention to woodwork, doors, and windows. If the home was constructed before 1978, or if the paint or underlying surface is deteriorating, you should have the paint tested for lead before renovating.

# Front Door

**YES / NO**

_____Is the doorbell broken?

_____Does the door lack weather stripping?

_____Is the door hardware broken or look worn out?

*Replacement cost: $300–$1,600, excluding hardware and based on a pre-hung installation*

# Garage Door

**YES / NO**

_____Is the garage door manual?

_____If the garage door is automatic, does it lack safety sensors?

*Note: Sensors detect obstructions and are a valuable safety feature.*

_____Is there a problem with opening and closing the garage door?

_____Does the garage door lack pressure rating?

*Note: Pressure-rated garage doors are especially helpful in hurricane and high-wind areas.*

# Wooden Garage Door

**YES / NO**

_____Is the door sagging, warped, or rotted along its bottom edge?
*Replacement cost: $1,600*

# Metal Garage Door

**YES / NO**

_____Is the door dented, rusted, or corroded?
*Replacement cost: $1,200–$1,600*

# Sills and Trim

**YES / NO**

_____Are the windowsills soft or rotted out?
*Note: Check especially the lower corners.*
_____Are the door, window, and building trims cracked, weathered, or warped? If so, new trim will be needed.
*Replacement cost: $300–$1,000*

# Windows

**YES / NO**

_____Are the windows in need of replacement?
*Wood-clad replacement cost per insulated window: $950*
*Note: Although wood windows are expensive, they are considered the most appealing. Clad windows are a combination of interior wood and exterior aluminum or vinyl.*
*Aluminum replacement cost per insulated window: $500*
*Note: This price is for basic sliding window configuration.*
*Vinyl replacement cost per insulated window: $500*

# UTILITIES

## Water

**YES / NO**

_____Is the water main hard to access?

## Gas

**YES / NO**

_____Is the gas main hard to access?

# ELECTRICAL

**YES / NO**

_____Is the lighting in front of the house too dim? You should be able to see your way from the driveway to the front door on a dark night.

_____Does the property lack an energy-efficient lighting system?

*Note: There are many different energy-efficient, motion-sensor, and inexpensive individual solar lights for walkways now available.*

_____Is the main electrical service panel equipped with fuses? Be aware that fuse panels are an antiquated electrical system, generally inadequate for today's modern electrical demands. Typically, a fuse panel has an amperage of 60 amps, whereas a 100-amp service is ideal.

*Replacement cost: $800–$1,200*

_____If the main electric service panel is on circuit breakers, is the service capacity less than 100 amps? Again, a capacity of 100 amps is ideal for today's modern demands.

*Replacement cost: $800–$1,200*

# The Front of the House Notes

# The Back of the House

Stroll out toward the back of the house. The backyard area also presents maintenance and convenience issues that you can not afford to ignore. Here are few things you need to check out:

## Fences and Walls

**YES / NO**

\_\_\_\_\_Are the fences and gates sagging rather than supporting?

\_\_\_\_\_Is the backyard not fully enclosed with fencing?

\_\_\_\_\_Do the fencing and walls fail to coincide with the actual property lines? If so, replacement or realignment may be in order.

\_\_\_\_\_Is there an overgrowth of bushes, vines, or plants on or next to the fence?

\_\_\_\_\_Are the gates difficult to open and close?

*Replacement cost: $30 per linear foot*

## Patio

**YES / NO**

\_\_\_\_\_If the patio is covered, is the cover sagging or leaking?

\_\_\_\_\_Is there any dry rot at the patio support post bases?

*Replacement cost: $150 per post base*

\_\_\_\_\_If the patio is of concrete, is the concrete cracked or separating?

*Replacement cost: $8 per square foot*

# DECK

**YES / NO**

_____If the deck is made of wood or composite ( Fiberon, TimberTech, EverGrain, Trex, Azek, and others) are the boards sagging? Are screws or nails missing? Is it weathered or rotted?

_____Are the support posts for the deck in contact with the ground? Contact between wood and soil leads to rot.

*Replacement cost: $35 per square foot*

_____Is the deck fifteen years old or older? Deck appearances can be deceiving.

# PATIO DOOR

**YES / NO**

_____Is there no screen door in addition to the patio door?

_____Is the door uninsulated?

_____Is the door difficult to open and close?

_____Is the door itself in poor condition?

_____Is the door hardware broken, or does it look worn out?

_____Do the inside corners of the door at the floor level show signs of leakage?

*Replacement cost: $1,200–$1,500*

# EXTERIOR LIGHTING

**YES / NO**

_____Is the lighting inadequate? You should have enough lighting to entertain guests in your backyard at night.

_____Are the light switches placed inconveniently?

_____Does the exterior lighting lack motion sensors?

# Sills and Trim

**YES / NO**

_____Are the windowsills soft or rotted out?
*Note: Check especially the lower corners.*
_____Are the door, window, and building trims cracked, weathered, or warped? If so, new trim will be needed.
*Replacement cost: $300–$1,000*
*Note: Older (1978 and prior) homes may contain lead-based paint.* Lead was used in oil-based paints. Latex water-based paints generally do not contain lead. The majority of the homes built between 1940 and 1978 contain leaded paint. It could be on any interior or exterior surface; pay close attention to woodwork, doors, and windows. If the home was constructed before 1978, or if the paint or underlying surface is deteriorating, you should have the paint tested for lead before renovating.

# Windows

**YES / NO**

_____Are the windows in need of replacement?
*Wood-clad, vinyl-clad, and aluminum-clad replacement cost per insulated window: $950*
*Note: Clad windows are a combination of interior wood and exterior aluminum or vinyl. Aluminum replacement cost per window: $500*
*Note: This price is for a basic sliding insulated window configuration.*
*Vinyl replacement cost per window: $500*
*Note: This price is for a basic sliding insulated window configuration.*

# RETAINING WALL

**YES / NO**

\_\_\_\_\_Is the wall sagging or unstable?

\_\_\_\_\_If the wall is made of wood, is the wood rotted?

*Replacement cost is dependent upon how many cubic yards of earth need to be removed in order to replace the wall—get an estimate.*

\_\_\_\_\_Is the wall made of concrete block?

\_\_\_\_\_Is there any separation, sagging, or missing blocks?

*Replacement cost is dependent upon how many cubic yards of earth need to be removed in order to replace*
*the concrete blocks—get an estimate.*

# LANDSCAPING

**YES / NO**

\_\_\_\_\_If there is a sprinkler system, is it inoperable?

\_\_\_\_\_Is the water pressure from the faucets too low?

\_\_\_\_\_Is the landscaping poorly maintained or simply unattractive?

\_\_\_\_\_Are there insufficient walkways? You should be able to navigate the backyard comfortably even after heavy rains.

\_\_\_\_\_Is there any evidence of pooling of water? If so, there may be flooding problems during the rainy season.

# Jacuzzi and Swimming Pool

**YES / NO**

_____Does the pool or Jacuzzi appear shabby or neglected? Inspect the entire area.

_____Are operating instructions unavailable?

_____Are the electrical outlets not GFCIs (Ground Fault Circuit Interrupters)? GFCI outlets have built-in fuses for safety.

_____Is there no heating system?

_____If there is a heating system, is it inoperable?

_____Is the area lack childproofing? A fence around the pool or Jacuzzi is a good precaution.

_____Does the Jacuzzi lack a locking cover?

_____Is the Jacuzzi and the surrounding structure code compliant?

*Note: If the Jacuzzi is independent and free-standing, check the support base to see if there are any cracks or separation. If there are any signs of deterioration, get an estimate.*

# Sewage

**YES / NO**

_____Is the house connected to the city sewage system?

_____Does the house have a septic tank requiring excessive maintenance?

*Septic tanks must be pumped out from time to time. Smaller tanks must be pumped out more frequently.*

*Service fee for pumping out a septic tank: $225*

# The Back of the House Notes

# Roof and Foundation

We've covered a lot of territory regarding the exterior of the home, and you may be itching to go inside now and look at the living space! Patience. There are still two more important, expensive parts of the house we need to attend to while we're outside: the roof and the foundation.

You may not have access to the roof; however, you need to find out the following information.

## Roofs

There are six basic types of roofing materials, each raising a different set of questions.

# Asphalt Composition Shingle

This is the most common type of roof. The life expectancy of an asphalt composition shingle roof is twenty-five to fifty years. *Find out how old the roof is.*

**YES / NO**

_____Are the shingles curled rather than flat?

_____Is there an area where the shingles appear to be a different color? This most likely reflects a patch job and suggests general roof deterioration.

_____Is there more than one layer of roofing material? Two roofing layers is the maximum due to considerations of weight.

_____If there is more than one layer of shingles and the roof is more than fifteen years old, does the roof have a weathered appearance or can you see mildew or moss? If so, you need a new roof.

*Estimated cost to remove the old roof and install a new asphalt composite roof: $12,000–$20,000*

# Wood Shake

The life expectancy of a wood shake roof is twenty to thirty years. *Find out how old the roof is.*

**YES / NO**

_____Are the shingles split, missing, or rotted? If so, you need a new roof.

_____Is the metal flashing rusted at the valley connecting roof angles? If so, you may need a new roof.

_____Do the shingles lack fire retardant? Without fire retardant, a wood shake roof is a fire hazard. By mere visual inspection, you cannot tell whether shingles have been treated, so you must ask the seller and, if possible, get proof.

*Estimated replacement cost: $20,000*

## Tar and Gravel

This kind of roof can be a little tricky, because it is most often flat. Therefore, you generally cannot see the roof from ground level. This could be a contingency item based on further examination. The life expectancy of a tar-and-gravel roof is fifteen to twenty years. *Find out how old the roof is.*

**YES / NO**

_____Is there severe blistering on the surface of the roof? If so, you need a new roof.

_____Are there areas where the tar is cracked and weathered? If so, you need a new roof.

*Estimated replacement cost: $10,000*

## Slate and Concrete Tiles

If the house has this kind of roof and it has been properly installed, you are in luck! This type of roof is extremely durable. The life expectancy of most slate or concrete tile roofs is forty years or more. *Find out how old the roof is.*

**YES / NO**

_____Is the roof sagging? (Slate is heavy.) If so, roofing replacement and other repairs are called for.

*Estimated replacement cost: $20,000*

# Torch On

A "torch on" roof is one that is made up of tar paper roll or bitumen membrane sheets and applied with hot tar. The tar is softened and melted into place by propane torches.

**YES / NO**

_____Is there severe blistering on the surface of the roof? If so, you need a new roof.

_____Are there areas where the tar is cracked and weathered? If so, you need a new roof.

*Estimated replacement cost: $10,000*

# Roof Line

**YES / NO**

_____Are the exterior rafter vents rotted out?

*Replacement cost per vent: $35*

_____Is the roof line sagging? If so, there is a serious defect in the roof's underlying framing. More than a mere replacement of roofing material is required.

*Replacement costs can vary—get an estimate.*

_____Do the ends of the rafters at the rim of the roof look rotted? This, too, may indicate a serious defect in the roof's underlying framing.

*Replacement costs can vary—get an estimate.*

# Fireplace and Chimney

**YES / NO**

_____Is the top of the chimney missing a spark arrestor?
*Estimated cost: $250–$500*
A spark arrestor is visible from the ground ***and is often made of metal with a single horizontal opening that covers the top of the chimney***

If the fireplace foundation is visible, does it appear to be in poor condition? It is always a good idea to have the fireplace inspected.

_____Does the fireplace brick and mortar show signs of cracking or crumbling?
*Replacement costs can vary—get an estimate.*

# Gutters and Downspouts

**YES / NO**

_____Are the gutters sagging? If so, you need new gutters.

_____Are the bottoms of the gutters rusted out? If so, you need new gutters.

_____Are the gutter downspouts clogged and/or draining improperly? A quick water test will tell you; spray some water from a garden hose, if available, into the gutters.
*Estimated replacement cost: $900–$2,200*
*Note: Seamless aluminum is ideal.*

# Foundation

_____If the foundation is of concrete, are there numerous lateral cracks in it? Lateral cracks signify a serious problem.

_____If the foundation is of concrete, are there no anchor bolts tying the house's wooden frame to it? This is easy to check; if the interior garage walls are exposed (no sheetrock), you should be able to see these bolts at the meeting place between walls and foundation.

_____Are there no downspouts in place that route the water away from the property?

_____If the house was built prior to 1960, ask and make sure that there are foundation bolts in place.

_____If the house is on a raised, perimeter foundation with suspended, wooden floor joists, is there a great deal of moisture present? This moisture may indicate poor cross ventilation, which is likely to promote decay in the wood.

_Note: You may have to access this area from inside the house, depending on the layout._

## Foundations are Fundamental

If the foundation is in poor condition (separated at the corners, severely cracked or undermined where the bottom of the foundation is exposed, etc.), _you may want to move on to another house._

# Roof and Foundation Notes

# The Interior of
# the House

Finally, it is time to step inside the house. Take a look around. If you are like most prospective home buyers, your immediate thoughts on the space have to do with what it will be like to live there. In what manner will you furnish the house? Does the house's look and feel fit your lifestyle and personal tastes? These questions are perfectly legitimate, and the answers should undoubtedly play a role in your decision-making process.

However, they should only be part of the equation. Remember, buying a home isn't just an aesthetic or lifestyle decision; it's also a very important economic one. The time has come to view the house's living space in an objective, sensible, and critical light. Look at the overall situation from your pocketbook's perspective and ask the question, "How much is this house really going to cost me?"

# Front Hall and Foyer

**First Impression**

_____
_____
_____
_____
_____
_____
_____
_____
_____
_____
_____
_____
_____
_____

## YES / NO

_____Does front foyer or hall have any distinctive odors?
*Note: Ask the seller to disclose any mold, mildew, or water-related problems.* Some states require sellers to disclose information about mold. The seller's duty to disclose only relates to what the seller knows about or reasonably should know about; the seller does not have a duty to open up walls or floors to see if there is mold. If you believe there is mold, *get an estimate.*

# FLOOR

**YES / NO**

_____If the flooring is of carpet, are there stained, discolored, worn, or matted areas?
Replacement cost: $15 - $25 per square yard
_____If the flooring is of hardwood, are there scratched, gouged, discolored, worn, or patched areas?
*Replacement cost: $12 - $15 per square foot*
_____If the flooring is of tile, are there cracks in the tile or is the grout popping out?
*Replacement cost: $7–$12 per square foot*
_____If the flooring is of vinyl, is its pattern unattractive?
_____If the flooring is of vinyl, are there bubbles or flaps where the material has detached from the subfloor?
*Replacement cost: $8 per square foot*
_____If the flooring is of laminate, is it buckling in any areas or coming apart?
_____If the flooring is of laminate, are there any scratched, gouged, discolored, worn, or patched areas?
*Replacement cost: $7–$12 per square foot*

# HEATING

**YES / NO**

_____Does the area lack a heating vent? The heating vent should be on the floor, low on a wall, or on the ceiling.
*Note: No heating vents may signify no central heating—ask the seller.*
_____If there is insulation, is it asbestos based?
*Note: Houses built prior to the mid-1960s may have asbestos as insulation wrap on heating ducts.* If in doubt, have it sampled and analyzed by a qualified professional.

If asbestos material is more than slightly damaged, or if you are going to make changes in the home that might disturb it, repair or removal by a professional is recommended. Before you have your house remodeled, find out whether asbestos materials are present.

# Leaks

**YES / NO**

_____Are there any discolorations on the ceiling? If so, there may be a roof leak—*get an estimate.*

_____If there is wallpaper, is it peeling? If so, this, too, may indicate a leak.

*Note: Ask the seller to disclose any mold, mildew, or water-related problems.* Some states require sellers to disclose information about mold. The seller's duty to disclose only relates to what the seller knows about or reasonably should know about; the seller does not have a duty to open up walls or floors to see if there is mold. If you believe there is mold, *get an estimate.*

# Lighting

**YES / NO**

_____Is the overhead lighting poorly located or outdated?

_____Is the lighting dim?

_____Are the light switches inconveniently located?

_____Is the natural light inadequate in the daytime?

*Note: You shouldn't have to resort to electrical light during the day.*

# Coat Closet

**YES / NO**

_____If the closet is located on a perimeter wall, is there mildew on the wall?

*Cost of repaint with fungicidal additive: $2 per square foot*

_____Is the shelving flimsy or otherwise defective?

_____Is the clothes rack flimsy or otherwise defective?

_____Is the lighting dim?

_____Is the light switch inconveniently located?

# Smoke Detector

## YES / NO

_____If the area requires a smoke detector, is there no smoke detector in the area?

*Replacement cost: $10–$30*

_____If there is a smoke detector, is it hardwired?

*Note: A hardwired smoke detector is directly connected to a 110-volt electrical outlet; batteries for this type of unit are not needed.* If you press the test button on the smoke detector and the alarm sounds and there are no batteries to change, the detector is hardwired.

# Wall Surfaces

## YES / NO

_____Is the paint cracking, peeling, or discolored?

*Repainting costs: $2 per square foot*

*Note: Older (1978 and prior) homes may contain lead-based paint.* Lead was used in oil-based paints. Latex water-based paints generally do not contain lead. The majority of the homes built between 1940 and 1978 contain leaded paint. It could be on any interior or exterior surface; pay close attention to woodwork, doors, and windows. If the home was constructed before 1978, or if the paint or underlying surface is deteriorating, you should have the paint tested for lead before renovating.

_____If there is wallpaper, is it peeling or discolored?

*Hanging wallpaper cost: $1 per square foot*

# Look Out for Skylights

If the house happens to have skylights:

**YES / NO**

_____Are there dark discolorations in the ceiling around the skylight? If so, *get an estimate.*

_____If the skylight is made of acrylic, is there any cracking, discoloration, or indication of leakage?

*Replacement cost for acrylic skylight: $350–$400*

_____If the skylight is made of glass, are there signs of leakage?

*Replacement cost for glass skylight: $500*

*Note: Any overhead glass window must be of tempered glass.* You can always recognize a tempered glass window by the small, noticeable icon on the lower corner of the glass.

# Front Hall and Foyer Notes

# LIVING ROOM

**First Impression**

_____
_____
_____
_____
_____
_____
_____
_____
_____
_____
_____
_____

## YES / NO

_____Does this area have any distinctive odors?

*Note: Ask the seller to disclose any mold, mildew, or water-related problems.* Some states require sellers to disclose information about mold. The seller's duty to disclose only relates to what the seller knows about or reasonably should know about; the seller does not have a duty to open up walls or floors to see if there is mold. If you believe there is mold, *get an estimate.*

# Doors

**YES / NO**

_____Are the doors difficult to open and close?

_____Do the doors show signs of wear?

_____Is the door hardware broken or does it appear worn out?

_____Are there any cracks in the walls near the upper corners of the door openings?

*Replacement cost: $850 per complete interior door assembly*

# Electrical

**YES / NO**

_____Are there an insufficient number of electrical outlets?

*Note: If a room is ten-by-ten feet, the standard number of outlets is four.* They should be placed six feet from any wall and twelve feet from any other outlet.

_____Do the electrical outlets lack grounding? If the outlets do not accept three-pronged electrical plugs, *get an estimate.*

*Note: Some installations require a grounding wire to all plugs.* This could be expensive if they are not already in place.

# FIREPLACE

## First Impression

_____
_____
_____
_____
_____
_____
_____

## YES / NO

_____Is the fireplace mantel warped?

_____Does the underside of the fireplace mantel show signs of heat damage?

_____Is the fireplace hearth discolored, or is it separated from the floor or the fireplace?

*Replacement costs can vary—get an estimate.*

_____If the hearth is made of tile, is the tile cracked or is the grout popping out or missing in areas?

*Replacement cost: $10–$20 per square foot*

_____Are the fireplace box, damper, and/or flue in poor condition?

*Note: If so, have the entire system inspected before use—get an estimate.*

# Floor

**YES / NO**

\_\_\_\_\_If the flooring is of carpet, are there stained, discolored, worn, or matted areas?
*Replacement cost: $15–$25 per square yard*
\_\_\_\_\_If the flooring is of hardwood, are there scratched, gouged, discolored, or worn areas?
*Replacement cost: $12–$15 per square foot*
\_\_\_\_\_If the flooring is of tile, are there cracks in the tile or is the grout popping out?
*Replacement cost: $7–$12 per square foot*
\_\_\_\_\_If the flooring is of laminate, are there scratched, gouged, discolored, or worn areas?
*Replacement cost: $7 - $12per square foot*

# Heating

**YES / NO**

Does the area lack a heating vent? The heating vent should be on the floor, low on a wall, or on the ceiling.
*Note: No heating vents may signify no central heating—ask the seller.*
\_\_\_\_\_If there is insulation, is it asbestos based?
*Note: Houses built prior to the mid-1960s may have asbestos as insulation wrap on heating ducts.* If in doubt, have it sampled and analyzed by a qualified professional.

If asbestos material is more than slightly damaged, or if you are going to make changes in the home that might disturb it, repair or removal by a professional is recommended. Before you have your house remodeled, find out whether asbestos materials are present.

# Leaks

**YES / NO**

_____Does the ceiling show a dark discoloration?
*Note: If so, there may be a leak in the roof—get an estimate.*
_____If there is wallpaper, is it peeling anywhere?
*Note: If so, there may be a leak. Ask the seller to disclose any mold, mildew, or water-related problems.* Some states require sellers to disclose information about mold. The seller's duty to disclose only relates to what the seller knows about or reasonably should know about; the seller does not have a duty to open up walls or floors to see if there is mold. If you believe there is mold, *get an estimate.*

# Lighting

**YES / NO**

_____Is the overhead lighting poorly located or outdated?
_____Is the lighting dim?
_____Are the light switches inconveniently located?
_____Is the natural light inadequate in the daytime?
*Note: You shouldn't have to resort to electrical light during the day.*

# Windows

**YES / NO**

_____Is it difficult to open and close the windows?
_____Are there any wall cracks at the corners of windows?
*Note: If the cracks are minor, they can be repaired at time of painting.*
*Wood-clad replacement cost per insulated window: $950*
*Aluminum replacement cost per insulated window: $500*
*Vinyl replacement cost per insulated window: $500*

# Furnishings

**YES / NO**

_____Will you have difficulty fitting your furnishings into this room?

# Wall Surfaces

**YES / NO**

_____Is the paint cracking, peeling, or discolored?
*Repainting cost: $2 per square foot*
*Note: Older (1978 and prior) homes may contain lead-based paint.* Lead was used in oil-based paints. Latex water-based paints generally do not contain lead. The majority of the homes built between 1940 and 1978 contain leaded paint. It could be on any interior or exterior surface; pay close attention to woodwork, doors, and windows. If the home was constructed before 1978, or if the paint or underlying surface is deteriorating, you should have the paint tested for lead before renovating.
_____If there is wallpaper, is it peeling or discolored?
*Hanging wallpaper cost: $1 per square foot*
_____Are there cracks at the corners of the walls above windows or doors?
*Repair: If the cracks and splits in the wall are minor, they may be repaired at time of painting.*

# Living Room Notes

# Dining Room

**First Impression**

_____

_____

_____

_____

_____

_____

_____

**YES / NO**

_____Does this area have any distinctive odors?

_Note: Ask the seller to disclose any mold, mildew, or water-related problems._ Some states require sellers to disclose information about mold. The seller's duty to disclose only relates to what the seller knows about or reasonably should know about; the seller does not have a duty to open up walls or floors to see if there is mold. If you believe there is mold, _get an estimate._

# Electrical

## YES / NO

_____Are there an insufficient number of electrical outlets?
*Note: If a room is ten-by-ten feet, the standard number of outlets is four.* They should be placed six feet from any wall and twelve feet from any other outlet.

_____Do the electrical outlets lack grounding? If the outlets do not accept three-pronged electrical plugs, *get an estimate.*
*Note: Some installations require a grounding wire to all plugs.* They could be expensive if they are not already in place.

# Floor

## YES / NO

_____ If the flooring is of carpet, are there stained, discolored, worn, or matted areas?
*Replacement cost: $15–$25 per square yard*

_____ If the flooring is of hardwood, are there scratched, gouged, discolored, worn, or patched areas?
*Replacement cost: $12–$15 per square foot*

_____If the flooring is of tile, are there cracks in the tile, or is the grout popping out?
*Replacement cost: $7–$12 per square foot*

_____ If the flooring is of laminate, are there any scratched, gouged, discolored, worn, or patched areas?
*Replacement cost: $7-$12 per square foot*

# Heating

**YES / NO**

Does the area lack a heating vent? The heating vent should be on the floor, low on a wall, or on the ceiling.

*Note: No heating vents may signify no central heating—ask the seller.*

_____ If there is insulation, is it asbestos based?

*Note: Houses built prior to the mid-1960s may have asbestos as insulation wrap on heating ducts.* If in doubt, have it sampled and analyzed by a qualified professional.

If asbestos material is more than slightly damaged, or if you are going to make changes in the home that might disturb it, repair or removal by a professional is recommended. Before you have your house remodeled, find out whether asbestos materials are present.

# Leaks

**YES / NO**

_____ Does the ceiling show a dark discoloration?

*Note: If so, there may be a leak in the roof—get an estimate.*

_____ If there is wallpaper, is it peeling anywhere? If so, there may be a leak.

*Note: Ask the seller to disclose any mold, mildew, or water-related problems.* Some states require sellers to disclose information about mold. The seller's duty to disclose only relates to what the seller knows about or reasonably should know about; the seller does not have a duty to open up walls or floors to see if there is mold. If you believe there is mold, *get an estimate.*

# Lighting

**YES / NO**

_____Is the overhead lighting poorly located or outdated?
_____Is the lighting dim?
_____Are the light switches inconveniently located?
_____Is the natural light inadequate in the daytime?
*Note: You shouldn't have to resort to electrical light during the day.*

# Windows

**YES / NO**

_____Is it difficult to open and close the windows?
_____Are there any wall cracks at the corners of windows?
*Note: If the cracks are minor, they can be repaired at time of painting.*
*Wood-clad replacement cost per insulated window: $950*
*Aluminum replacement cost per insulated window: $500*
*Vinyl replacement cost per insulated window: $500*

# Wall Surfaces

**YES / NO**

_____Is the paint cracking, peeling, or discolored?
*Repainting cost: $2 per square foot*
*Note: Older (1978 and prior) homes may contain lead-based paint.* Lead was used in oil-based paints. Latex water-based paints generally do not contain lead. The majority of the homes built between 1940 and 1978 contain leaded paint. It could be on any interior or exterior surface; pay close attention to woodwork, doors, and windows. If the home was constructed before 1978, or if the paint or underlying surface is deteriorating, you should have the paint tested for lead before renovating.
_____If there is wallpaper, is it peeling or discolored?
*Hanging wallpaper cost: $1 per square foot*
_____Are there cracks at the corners of the walls above windows or doors?
*Repair: If cracks and splits in the wall are minor, they may be repaired at time of painting.*

# Thermostat

**YES / NO**

_____Is the thermostat not programmable?
_____Is the thermostat broken?

# Dining Room Notes

# KITCHEN

This is the most expensive room in the house. Pay special attention here! When it comes to repair, replacement, or upgrades, you will spend most of your time in this room.

**First Impression**

_____

_____

_____

_____

_____

_____

_____

## APPLIANCES

**YES / NO**

_____Are the appliances broken? You should test all appliances to be sure that they function properly.
*Replacement costs can vary—get prices for the desired appliances.*
_____Are the appliances outdated and/or not energy efficient?
_____Is the exhaust fan broken?
*Replacement cost: $300*
_____Have the warrantees on any or all appliances expired?
*Note: Ask the seller.*

# Cabinets

**YES / NO**

\_\_\_\_\_Are the cabinets antiquated, sagging, or simply unattractive?
\_\_\_\_\_Do the cabinet doors lack the feature of being self-closing?
\_\_\_\_\_Are the shelves fixed rather than adjustable?
\_\_\_\_\_Are the handles and hinges broken or worn out?
*Cabinet replacement cost: $110 per foot for base cabinets and $90 per linear foot for wall-mounted cabinets.*

# Countertops

**YES / NO**

\_\_\_\_\_If the countertop is of formica, are there cracks, burn marks, discolorations, or worn areas?
*Replacement cost: $25 per linear foot*
\_\_\_\_\_If the countertop is of ceramic tile, are there any cracks in the tile, or is it the grout popping out? Cracking is especially likely to occur where the wall meets the countertop.
*Replacement cost: $33–$55 per linear foot*
\_\_\_\_\_If the counter is of Corian, are there any discolorations or cracks at the sink area?
*Replacement cost: $50–$75 per linear foot*
\_\_\_\_\_If the countertop is of solid granite or other composite material, are there any cracks present?
*Replacement cost: $75–$100 per linear foot*

# Electrical

**YES / NO**

_____Are the electrical outlets around the countertop *not* GFCIs? GFCI (Ground Fault Circuit Interrupter) outlets have built-in fuses for safety, and they are a code requirement in modern kitchens.

_____Are there an insufficient number of outlets?

*Note: If a room is ten-by-ten feet, the standard number of outlets is four.* They should be placed six feet from any wall and twelve feet from any other outlet.

_____Do the electrical outlets lack grounding? If the outlets do not accept three-pronged electrical plugs, *get an estimate.*

*Note: Some installations require a grounding wire to all plugs.* They could be expensive if they are not already in place.

# Faucet and Sink

**YES / NO**

_____If the sink is a surface mount, is it cracked or discolored?

*Replacement cost: $300–$1,000*

_____If the sink is an undermount, is it cracked or discolored?

*Note: Be aware that undermount sinks are not replaceable without changing the whole countertop.*

_____Is the faucet leaky or otherwise defective?

*Replacement cost: $150–$500*

_____Is the garbage disposal broken?

*Replacement cost: $300*

# Floor

**YES / NO**

_____If the flooring is of hardwood, are there scratched, gouged, discolored, worn, or patched areas?
*Replacement cost: $12–$15 per square foot*
_____If the flooring is of tile, are there cracks in the tile, or is the grout popping out?
*Replacement cost: $7–$12 per square foot*
_____If the flooring is of laminate, are there any scratched, gouged, discolored, worn, or patched areas?
*Replacement cost: $7-$12 per square foot*
_____If the flooring is of vinyl, is its pattern unattractive?
_____If the flooring is of vinyl, are there bubbles or flaps where the material has detached from the subfloor?
*Replacement cost: $8 per square foot*

# Leaks

**YES / NO**

_____Does the ceiling show a dark discoloration?
*Note: If so, there may be a leak in the roof—get an estimate.*
_____If there is wallpaper, is it peeling anywhere?
*Note: If so, there may be a leak. Ask the seller to disclose any mold, mildew, or water-related problems.* Some states require sellers to disclose information about mold. The seller's duty to disclose only relates to what the seller knows about or reasonably should know about; the seller does not have a duty to open up walls or floors to see if there is mold. If you believe there is mold, *get an estimate.*

# Lighting

**YES / NO**

_____Is the overhead lighting poorly located or outdated?
_____Is the lighting dim?
_____Are the light switches inconveniently located?
_____Is the natural light inadequate in the daytime?
*Note: You shouldn't have to resort to electrical light during the day.*

# Pantry

**YES / NO**

_____Is the lighting dim?
_____Are the shelves fixed rather than adjustable?
_____Is there insufficient storage?

# Plumbing

**YES / NO**

_____Are there signs of leakage in the cabinet underneath the sink?
_____Are the water pipes galvanized rather than copper?
*Note: Galvanized pipes are problematic.*
*Replacement cost to upgrade to all copper pipe: $3,000–$6,000*

# Windows

**YES / NO**

_____Is it difficult to open and close the windows?
_____Are there any wall cracks at the corners of windows?
*Note: If the cracks are minor, they can be repaired at time of painting.*
*Wood-clad replacement cost per insulated window: $950*
*Aluminum replacement cost per insulated window: $500*
*Vinyl replacement cost per insulated window: $500*

# Wall Surfaces

## YES / NO

_____Is the paint cracking, peeling, or discolored?
*Repainting cost: $2 per square foot*
*Note: If the cracks are minor, they can be repaired at time of painting.* If they are larger and easily visible, *get an estimate.*
_____If there is wallpaper, is it peeling or discolored?
*Hanging wallpaper cost: $1 per square foot*
_____Are there cracks at the corners above windows or doors?
*Note: If the cracks are minor, they can be repaired at time of painting.* If they are larger and easily visible, *get an estimate.*

# Kitchen Notes

# Family Room and Breakfast Nook

**First Impression**

_____

_____

_____

_____

_____

_____

_____

## Electrical

**YES / NO**

_____Are there an insufficient number of electrical outlets?
*Note: If a room is ten-by-ten feet, the standard number of outlets is four.*
They should be placed six feet from any wall and twelve feet from any other outlet.

_____Do the electrical outlets lack grounding? If the outlets do not accept three-pronged electrical plugs, *get an estimate.*
*Note: Some installations require a grounding wire to all plugs.* They could be expensive if they are not already in place.

# Floor

**YES / NO**

_____If the flooring is of carpet, are there stained, discolored, worn, or matted areas?
*Replacement cost: $15–$25 per square foot*
_____If the flooring is of hardwood, are there scratched, gouged, discolored, worn, or patched areas?
*Replacement cost: $12–$15 per square foot*
_____If the flooring is of tile, are there cracks in the tile, or is the grout popping out?
*Replacement cost: $7–$12 per square foot*
_____If the flooring is of laminate, are there any scratched, gouged, discolored, worn, or patched areas?
*Replacement cost: $7-$12 per square foot*
_____If the flooring is of vinyl, is its pattern unattractive?
_____If the flooring is of vinyl, are there bubbles or flaps where the material has detached from the subfloor?
*Replacement cost: $8 per square foot*

# Heating

**YES / NO**

Does the area lack a heating vent? The heating vent should be on the floor, low on a wall, or on the ceiling.
*Note: No heating vents may signify no central heating—ask the seller.*
_____ If there is insulation, is it asbestos based?
*Note: Houses built prior to the mid-1960s may have asbestos as insulation wrap on heating ducts.* If in doubt, have it sampled and analyzed by a qualified professional.

If asbestos material is more than slightly damaged, or if you are going to make changes in the home that might disturb it, repair or removal by a professional is recommended. Before you have your house remodeled, find out whether asbestos materials are present.

# Leaks

**YES / NO**

\_\_\_\_\_Does the ceiling show a dark discoloration?
*Note: If so, there may be a leak in the roof—get an estimate.*
\_\_\_\_\_If there is wallpaper, is it peeling anywhere? If so, there may be a leak.
*Note: Ask the seller to disclose any mold, mildew, or water-related problems.* Some states require sellers to disclose information about mold. The seller's duty to disclose only relates to what the seller knows about or reasonably should know about; the seller does not have a duty to open up walls or floors to see if there is mold. If you believe there is mold, *get an estimate.*

# Lighting

**YES / NO**

\_\_\_\_\_Is the overhead lighting poorly located or outdated?
\_\_\_\_\_Is the lighting dim?
\_\_\_\_\_Are the light switches inconveniently located?
\_\_\_\_\_Is the natural light inadequate in the daytime?
*Note: You shouldn't have to resort to electrical light during the day.*

# Windows

**YES / NO**

\_\_\_\_\_Is it difficult to open and close the windows?
\_\_\_\_\_Are there any wall cracks at the corners of windows?
*Note: If the cracks are minor, they can be repaired at time of painting.*
*Wood-clad replacement cost per insulated window: $950*
*Aluminum replacement cost per insulated window: $500*
*Vinyl replacement cost per insulated window: $500*

## Wall Surfaces

**YES / NO**

_____Is the paint cracking, peeling, or discolored?
*Repainting cost: $2 per square foot*
_____If there is wallpaper, is it peeling or discolored?
*Hanging wallpaper cost: $1 per square foot*
_____Are there cracks at the corners above windows or doors?
*Repair: If cracks and splits in the wall are minor, they may be repaired at time of painting.* If they are larger and easily visible, *get an estimate.*

# Family Room and Breakfast Nook Notes

# Laundry Room

## Appliances

**YES / NO**

_____Does the dryer lack a vent to an exterior wall?
_____Does the laundry room lack a gas hookup?
*Note: If so, get an estimate.*
_____If there is insulation, is it asbestos based?
*Note: Houses built prior to the mid-1960s may have asbestos as insulation wrap on heating ducts.* If in doubt, have it sampled and analyzed by a qualified professional.

If asbestos material is more than slightly damaged, or if you are going to make changes in the home that might disturb it, repair or removal by a professional is recommended. Before you have your house remodeled, find out whether asbestos materials are present.

# Door

**YES / NO**

_____Is the door difficult to open and close?

_____Is the door itself in poor condition?

_____Is the door hardware broken?

_____Are there any cracks in the walls near the upper corners of the door openings?

*Repair: If cracks and splits in the wall are minor, they may be repaired at time of painting.* If they are larger and easily visible, *get an estimate.*

*Replacement cost: $500 per complete door assembly*

# Electrical

**YES / NO**

_____Does the laundry room lack a 220-volt electric outlet for the dryer?

*If so, get an estimate.*

*Note: If a room is ten-by-ten feet, the standard number of outlets is four.* They should be placed six feet from any wall and twelve feet from any other outlet.

_____Do the electrical outlets lack grounding? If the outlets do not accept three-pronged electrical plugs, *get an estimate.*

*Note: Some installations require a grounding wire to all plugs.* They could be expensive if they are not already in place.

# Floor

**YES / NO**

_____If the flooring is of hardwood, are there scratched, gouged, discolored, worn, or patched areas?
*Replacement cost: $12–$15 per square foot*
_____If the flooring is of tile, are there cracks in the tile, or is the grout popping out?
*Replacement cost: $7–$12 per square foot*
_____If the flooring is of laminate, are there any scratched, gouged, discolored, worn, or patched areas?
*Replacement cost: $7-$12 per square foot*
_____If the flooring is of vinyl, is its pattern unattractive?
_____If the flooring is of vinyl, are there bubbles or flaps where the material has detached from the subfloor?
*Replacement cost: $8 per square foot*

# Plumbing

**YES / NO**

_____At the wash basin, does the faucet or drain fail to function properly?
*Replacement cost for a fiberglass wash basin and drain system: $200–$250*
*Replacement cost for faucet: $100*

# Windows

**YES / NO**

_____Is it difficult to open and close the windows?
_____Are there any wall cracks at the corners of windows?
*Note: If the cracks are minor, they can be repaired at time of painting.*
*Wood-clad replacement cost per insulated window: $950*
*Aluminum replacement cost per insulated window: $500*
*Vinyl replacement cost per insulated window: $500*

## Wall Surfaces

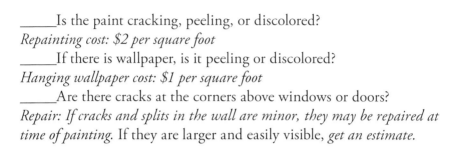

_____Is the paint cracking, peeling, or discolored?
*Repainting cost: $2 per square foot*
_____If there is wallpaper, is it peeling or discolored?
*Hanging wallpaper cost: $1 per square foot*
_____Are there cracks at the corners above windows or doors?
*Repair: If cracks and splits in the wall are minor, they may be repaired at time of painting.* If they are larger and easily visible, *get an estimate.*

# Laundry Room Notes

# Bedrooms

## Observations

How many bedrooms?

_____

_____

Is there a room to support hobbies or a telecommute office?

_____

_____

Is the master bedroom big enough for your furnishings?

_____

_____

Where are the bedrooms in relation to "traffic noise"?

_____

_____

Where does the sun rise and set in relation to the bedrooms?

_____

_____

# Closet

**YES / NO**

_____If the closet is located on a perimeter wall, is there mildew on the wall?
*Cost of repaint with fungicidal additive: $2 per square foot*
*Note: Ask the seller to disclose any mold, mildew, or water-related problems.* Some states require sellers to disclose information about mold. The seller's duty to disclose only relates to what the seller knows about or reasonably should know about; the seller does not have a duty to open up walls or floors to see if there is mold. If you believe there is mold, *get an estimate.*
_____Is the shelving flimsy or otherwise defective?
_____Is the clothes rack flimsy or otherwise defective?
_____Is the lighting dim?
_____Is the light switch inconveniently located?

# Doors

**YES / NO**

_____Are the doors difficult to open and close?
_____Are the doors themselves in poor condition?
_____Is the door hardware broken, or does it appear worn out?
_____Are there any cracks in the walls near the upper corners of the door openings?
*Repair: If cracks and splits in the wall are minor, they may be repaired at time of painting. If they are larger and easily visible, get an estimate.*
*Replacement cost: $500 per complete interior door assembly*

# Electrical

## YES / NO

_____Are there an insufficient number of electrical outlets?
*Note: If a room is ten-by-ten feet, the standard number of outlets is four.* They should be placed six feet from any wall and twelve feet from any other outlet.

_____Do the electrical outlets lack grounding? If the outlets do not accept three-pronged electrical plugs, *get an estimate.*
*Note: Some installations require a grounding wire to all plugs.* They could be expensive if they are not already in place.

_____Is there no CAD 5 wiring in the house?
*Note: CAD 5 wiring is often called Ethernet cable and is short for category 5 cable.* This cable is the current industry standard for network and telephone wiring.

# Floor

## YES / NO

_____If the flooring is of carpet, are there stained, discolored, worn, or matted areas?
*Replacement cost: $15–$25 per square yard*

_____If the flooring is of hardwood, are there scratched, gouged, discolored, worn, or patched areas?
*Replacement cost: $12–$15 per square foot*

_____If the flooring is of tile, are there cracks in the tile, or is the grout popping out?
*Replacement cost: $7–$12 per square foot*

_____If the flooring is of laminate, are there any scratched, gouged, discolored, worn, or patched areas?
*Replacement cost: $7-$12per square foot*

# Heating

**YES / NO**

Does the area lack a heating vent? The heating vent should be on the floor, low on a wall, or on the ceiling.
*Note: No heating vents may signify no central heating—ask the seller.*
*Note: Houses built prior to the mid-1960s may have asbestos as insulation wrap on heating ducts.* If in doubt, have it sampled and analyzed by a qualified professional.

If asbestos material is more than slightly damaged, or if you are going to make changes in the home that might disturb it, repair or removal by a professional is recommended. Before you have your house remodeled, find out whether asbestos materials are present.

# Leaks

**YES / NO**

_____Does the ceiling show a dark discoloration?
*Note: If so, there may be a leak in the roof—**get** an estimate.*
_____If there is wallpaper, is it peeling anywhere?
*Note: If so, there may be a leak. Ask the seller to disclose any mold, mildew, or water-related problems.* Some states require sellers to disclose information about mold. The seller's duty to disclose only relates to what the seller knows about or reasonably should know about; the seller does not have a duty to open up walls or floors to see if there is mold. If you believe there is mold, *get an estimate.*

# Lighting

**YES / NO**

_____Is the overhead lighting poorly located or outdated?
_____Is the lighting dim?
_____Are the light switches inconveniently located?
_____Is the natural light inadequate in the daytime?
*Note: You shouldn't have to resort to electrical light during the day.*

# Windows

**YES / NO**

_____Is it difficult to open and close the windows?

_____Are there any wall cracks at the corners of windows?

*Note: If the cracks are minor, they can be repaired at time of painting.*

*Wood-clad replacement cost per insulated window: $950*

*Aluminum replacement cost per insulated window: $500*

*Vinyl replacement cost per insulated window: $500*

# Wall Surfaces

**YES / NO**

_____Is the paint cracking, peeling, or discolored?

*Repainting cost: $2 per square foot*

_____If there is wallpaper, is it peeling or discolored?

*Hanging wallpaper cost: $1 per square foot*

_____Are there cracks at the corners above windows or doors?

*Note: If the cracks are minor, they can be repaired at time of painting.* If they are larger and easily visible, *get an estimate.*

# Bedrooms Notes

# Bathrooms

**This is the second-most expensive room in the house. Like the kitchen, a bathroom calls for special attention.**

## Ceiling

**YES / NO**

\_\_\_\_\_If the ceiling is blistered or shows signs of mildew, is the window or exhaust fan broken?

*Replacement cost for exhaust fan: $300–$500*

*Note: Ask the seller to disclose any mold, mildew, or water-related problems.* Some states require sellers to disclose information about mold. The seller's duty to disclose only relates to what the seller knows about or reasonably should know about; the seller does not have a duty to open up walls or floors to see if there is mold. If you believe there is mold, *get an estimate.*

# Door

**YES / NO**

_____Is the door difficult to open and close?

_____Is the door itself in poor condition?

_____Is the door's hardware broken?

_____Are there any cracks in the walls near the upper corners of the door opening?

*Note: If the cracks are minor, they can be repaired at time of painting.* If they are larger and easily visible, *get an estimate.*

*Replacement cost: $500 per complete interior door assembly*

# Electrical

**YES / NO**

_____Do the electrical outlets lack a grounding? The outlets should accept three-pronged electrical plugs.

_____Are there outlets in the bathroom that are *not* GFCIs? GFCI outlets are safer here. Look for a reset button at the center of the outlet.

_____Is there a need for more electrical outlets or wall switches?

*Note: Some installations require a grounding wire to all plugs.* The bathroom is a special area and may require more outlets for your needs. This could be expensive if not already in place. *Get an estimate.*

# Faucet and Sink

## YES / NO

_____Does the sink drain slowly?

_____Is the drain's pop-up valve broken?

_____Is the faucet dull or scratched?

*Replacement cost: $150–$300*

_____Does the faucet function inadequately?

_____Is the water pressure inadequate?

*Note: Flush the toilet and run the water from the bathroom faucet at the same time to see if there is a noticeable difference in faucet water pressure. If so, get an estimate.*

_____Is the wood at the base of the vanity warped? If so, this is an indication of previous water damage.

*Note: There may be a leak in the plumbing. Get an estimate.*

*Replacement cost for vanity base: $400–$800*

# Floor and Walls

## YES / NO

_____If the flooring is of tile, are there cracks in the tile, or is the grout popping out?

*Replacement cost: $7–$12 per square foot*

_____If the flooring is of vinyl, is its pattern unattractive?

_____If the flooring is of vinyl, are there bubbles or flaps where the material has detached from the subfloor?

*Replacement cost: $8 per square foot*

_____Immediately outside the bathtub enclosure, are there any signs of water damage to the floor or walls, or are there any signs that these areas have been recently repaired?

*Note: If so, you may have a shower leak, or maybe there is a fixture or valve that is leaking inside the shower enclosure walls—get an estimate.*

*Repair of wall: $200–$500*

*Replacement cost for underlayment and finish vinyl flooring: $20 per square foot*

# The Complete Bathroom Remodel

Bathroom repair has a tendency to snowball. This is due to the fact that so many of these repairs are interconnected. For instance, in order to change the bathtub, the bathtub surround (i.e., the materials immediately around the tub, including the tile and its backing) must also be replaced, for the chances of a new bathtub fitting properly in an existing surround area are virtually nonexistent.

For this reason, if the bathroom has been heavily used and looks run down, you should consider doing a complete remodel.

A basic, complete bathroom remodel includes replacement of toilet, underlayment, flooring, baseboards, tile backing material, tile, bathtub, shower door, tub and shower fixtures, waste and overflow on the bathtub, plumbing upgrades, vanity sink, vanity base, medicine cabinet, vanity lighting, overhead lighting, and paint.

*Cost of complete remodel: $5,000–$20,000 or even more depending on your tastes in décor*

## YES / NO

_____Are there cracks at the corners above windows or doors?
*Note: If the cracks are minor, they can be repaired at time of painting.* If they are larger and easily visible, *get an estimate.*
_____Is the paint cracking, peeling, or discolored?
*Repainting costs: $2 per square foot*
_____If there is wallpaper, is it peeling or discolored?
*Hanging wallpaper cost: $1 per square foot*

# Heating

**YES / NO**

_____Does the bathroom lack a heating system, such as a heating vent or ceiling heating unit?
*Note: No heating vents may signify no central heating—ask the seller.*
_____Is the ventilation fan operable?
*Note: Houses built prior to the mid-1960s may have asbestos as insulation wrap on heating ducts.* If in doubt, have it sampled and analyzed by a qualified professional.

If asbestos material is more than slightly damaged, or if you are going to make changes in the home that might disturb it, repair or removal by a professional is recommended. Before you have your house remodeled, find out whether asbestos materials are present.

# Lighting

**YES / NO**

_____Is the overhead lighting poorly located?
_____Is the overhead lighting dim?
_____Is the vanity lighting dim?
_____Are the light switches inconveniently located?
_____Is the natural light inadequate in the daytime?
*Note: You shouldn't have to resort to electrical lighting during the day.*

# Shower/Bath

**YES / NO**

_____If there is a window above the shower area, are there grout discolorations, or are the tiles on the
windowsill loose?
*Note: If so, we recommend a new tub surround.*
*Replacement cost: $1,000–$1,700*
_____Is it difficult to open and close the windows?
_____Are there any wall cracks at the corners of windows?
*Note: If the cracks are minor, they can be repaired at time of painting.*
*Wood-clad replacement cost per insulated window: $950*
*Aluminum replacement cost per insulated window: $500*
*Vinyl replacement cost per insulated window: $500*
_____Is the bathtub discolored, rusted, or dull in finish?

# ADDITIONAL TROUBLE

If there has been any significant remodeling or special room additions after the original construction of the home, ask to see the building permits. This way, you can be sure that the work was performed in accordance with the local building codes.

Check to see whether permits are currently available for remodels and add-ons. If not, this may be because of known problems with the house, such as wood and soil contact problems, faulty electrical wiring, substandard plumbing, poor roof tie-ins, or an unsafe foundation. These problems may prove to be too costly to fix, and you may want to move on to another house.

**YES / NO**

_____Does the waste and overflow valve function poorly, or does the bathtub drain slowly?
*Replacement cost for porcelain steel tub: $350–$500*
*Replacement cost for cast iron porcelain tub: $500–$1,000*
_____Are the tub and shower fixtures dull looking?
_____Do the fixtures leak or otherwise function inadequately?
*Replacement cost for tub and shower fixtures: $500–$1,250*
_____Do the tub fixtures appear scratched, abused, or dented?
*Note: If so, these fixtures may have been hastily rebuilt to sell the house.*
_____Is there an excessive amount of caulking where the tub meets the tile work, or are the tiles in this area loose or cracked? If so, water may be leaking into the walls surrounding the tub.
*Replacement cost for a new tiled tub surround: $1,500–$3,500*

# Toilet

**YES / NO**

_____Is the toilet constantly running?

_____Are the fixtures worn?

*Repair cost: $75–$250*

*Replacement cost: $250–$800*

_____Is the toilet loose on its mounting base? An easy way to check is to sit on the toilet and see whether it rocks back and forth. If it does, this could mean loose toilet bolts or a broken toilet hub—*get an estimate*.

*Note: Is the toilet a water saver (1.4-gallon flush)?* Your water usage and monthly water bill would be greatly reduced (older toilets are 3.0-gallon flush).

# Bathrooms Notes

# BASEMENT

At this point, you've covered all of the home's interior living space, and you have been very thorough in your inspection. So far, so good—at this point, you may be inclined to think that your walk-through should be over. After all, you're thinking, "Whatever remains inside the house is seldom seen, anyway. How could these areas possibly be important?"

Careful! What you don't see *can* cost you. In your next home, it can cost you dearly.

Step into the basement. Although homeowners typically spend little time here, a prospective home buyer can't afford to neglect this part of the house. What you find in this area could make the difference between buying and walking away.

**YES / NO**

_____Is there a damp smell?
*Note: Ask the seller to disclose any mold, mildew, or water-related problems.* Some states require sellers to disclose information about mold. The seller's duty to disclose only relates to what the seller knows about or reasonably should know about; the seller does not have a duty to open up walls or floors to see if there is mold. If you believe there is mold, *get an estimate.*

# Doors

**YES / NO**

\_\_\_\_\_Is the door difficult to open and close?

\_\_\_\_\_Is the door itself in poor condition?

\_\_\_\_\_Is the door's hardware broken?

\_\_\_\_\_Are there any cracks in the walls near the upper corners of the door openings?

*.Note: If the cracks are minor, they can be repaired at time of painting.* If they are larger and easily visible, *get an estimate.*

*Replacement cost: $500 per complete door assembly*

# Severe Weather Safety

**YES / NO**

\_\_\_\_\_If the overhead floor joist, beams, and posts are exposed, are the joints between them fortified with metal straps? Points of contact between distinct joists, beams, and posts are highly vulnerable to severe weather damage and should be amply reinforced.

*Note: Supporting posts and beams are especially important.*

\_\_\_\_\_Are the vertical posts not anchored to their concrete bases?

\_\_\_\_\_Are the wooden studs in the walls exposed and visible? Ideally, plywood sheets should be nailed to the stud walls—at least in some areas. This creates what is known as a "shear wall," and it greatly enhances the home's structural integrity.

\_\_\_\_\_Is there an absence of anchor bolts tying the house's walls to its concrete foundation? You should find these bolts running through the "mud-sill," which is the horizontal board at the bottom of the stud wall, lying directly on top of the foundation and underneath the vertical studs.

*Note 1: This is a very important question to ask, especially if the home is in an earthquake-prone area.*

*Note 2: To prevent rot or infestation, the mud-sill should be treated wood.*

You can recognize treated wood by its greenish or brownish tint and uniformly distributed puncture marks.

## FOUNDATION

**YES / NO**

_____Is the concrete floor severely cracked?

_____If there are partial- or full-height foundation walls along the perimeter of the basement, do they show signs of water penetration, or do they contain severe cracking, exposed steel, or crumbling?

_____Do the foundation walls lack steel rebar reinforcement?

## FRAMING

**YES / NO**

_____Is there evidence of rot in the exposed wood framing?

*Note: If so, get an estimate for repair.*

_____Are there piles of a brown granular substance anywhere near the stud walls? This probably indicates termites.

*Note: Ask to see the seller's termite and pest control report—or you may want to get your own.*

## LIGHTING

**YES / NO**

_____Is the lighting dim? You probably won't be spending a lot of time in your basement, but there should be enough light for you to view the entire space comfortably.

_____Are the light switches inconveniently located?

## STAIRCASE

**YES / NO**

_____Is the lighting in the stairwell inadequate?

_____Do the stairs sag?

_____Are the stairs cracked or rotted?

_____Are the handrails missing?

# Safe Room

_____Is there a safe room or reinforced area within the house in case of hurricanes, tornadoes, lightning, and/or hailstorms?
*Note: An area near the center of your house and below ground if possible— or at least on the lowest floor—is optimal.*

# Water Woes

## Moisture

*Note: The prolonged presence of moisture in the basement may lead to damage in the framing.* If moisture is present, there may be damage; check for the presence of rot. Have the basement inspected by a termite and pest professional.

**YES / NO**

_____Is there excessive moisture or evidence of water damage in the flooring?
_____Is there an elevated wooden floor over a concrete floor? This suggests that water penetrates the basement in times of rain.
_____Is the basement poorly ventilated?
*Note: Proper ventilation helps to expel the moisture.*

## Flooding

*Note: If you see evidence of flooding problems, it is absolutely imperative that you get a repair estimate.* The cost of such repairs can be high, but if flooding problems are neglected, extreme damage to the home can result.

**YES / NO**

_____If the basement is susceptible to flooding, is it impossible for water to drain out of the basement on its own?
*Note 1: Water should flow out, not pool up.* If there is inadequate drainage, there should at least be a sump pump rigged to start automatically in the event of flooding. Be sure that water from the pump discharges at a location clear of the house.
*Replacement cost for 110-volt sump pump: $300–$500*
*Note 2: The electrical for the sump pump must be a GFIC-rated outlet.*

# Garage and Utility Room

## Garage

## Cars

**YES / NO**

\_\_\_\_\_Is there insufficient room for your automobiles?

## Door (From garage to inside of house)

**YES / NO**

\_\_\_\_\_Is the door difficult to open and close?
\_\_\_\_\_Is the door itself in poor condition?
\_\_\_\_\_Is the door hollow? For fire safety reasons, this door should have a solid core.
\_\_\_\_\_Is the door's hardware broken?
\_\_\_\_\_Are there any cracks in the walls near the upper corners of the door opening?
*Replacement cost: $500 per complete interior door assembly*

# Electrical Outlets

**YES / NO**

_____Are there an insufficient number of electrical outlets?

_____Do the electrical outlets lack a grounding? The outlets should at least accept three-pronged electrical plugs.

*Note: Some installations require a grounding wire to all plugs. This could be expensive if not already in place—get an estimate.*

# Electrical Panel

*Note: There may be an electrical panel in this room. If so, open the panel door and inspect.*

**YES / NO**

_____Is the panel equipped with fuses? Be aware that fuse panels are an antiquated electrical system, generally inadequate for modern electrical demands.

*Note: Typically, a fuse panel has an amperage capacity of 60 amps, whereas 100-amp service is ideal.*

*Replacement cost: $800–$1,200*

_____If the panel is on circuit breakers, are there less than 100 amps of service capacity? Again, 100-amp service is ideal.

*Upgrade cost: $800–$1,200*

# Foundation

**YES / NO**

_____Are there severe cracks in the garage floor?

*Note: If so, there may be drainage or settling problems.*

_____If the perimeter foundation is visible, does it contain severe cracks?

_____If the perimeter foundation and wall studs are visible, is there an absence of anchor bolts tying the walls to the foundation?

_____Are there no downspouts in place that route the water away from the property?

# Lighting

_____Is the overhead lighting poorly located?
_____Is the lighting dim?
_____Are the light switches inconveniently located?

# Utility Room

The house may or may not have a utility room containing the items listed below. In any event, be sure to check the following:

## Furnace

**YES / NO**

_____Does the furnace run on oil?
_____If the furnace runs on gas, does it lack electronic ignition?
_____Are there no lighting instructions for the gas pilot light?
_____Is the main gas shutoff valve hard to access?
_____Is the disposable furnace filter hard to access?

*Gas furnace replacement cost: $2,800–$4,500*
*Note 1: This should be covered by a home warranty—ask the seller.*
*Note 2: All gas furnaces and gas hot water heaters need a combustible exit to function (i.e., proper ventilation).* All nonelectric furnaces emit carbon monoxide, so all exhaust vents must be in accordance uniform building codes.
*Note 3: Houses built prior to the mid-1960s may have asbestos as insulation wrap on heating ducts.* If in doubt, have it sampled and analyzed by a qualified professional.

If asbestos material is more than slightly damaged, or if you are going to make changes in the home that might disturb it, repair or removal by a professional is recommended. Before you have your house remodeled, find out whether asbestos materials are present.

# Air-Conditioning Unit

**YES / NO**

_____Is the air conditioner broken or defective? Try running it. Check to see whether it cools the house effectively.

*Note 1: If the air conditioner produces squeaky noises, there is a problem with the blower unit or belts. Get an estimate.*

*Replacement cost: $1,800–$2,800*

*Note 2: This should be covered by a home warranty—ask the seller.*

# Hot Water Heater

**YES / NO**

_____Is the hot water heater too small in capacity?

Note :As a general rule if the number of people, bathrooms and appliances is less than four, you need only a 30-gallon tank. If the number is between five and seven, you need a 50-gallon tank. If your number is eight or nine, you need a 80-gallon water heater.

_____Does the hot water heater run on electricity rather than gas?

*Note 1: Gas hot water heaters are more energy efficient.*

*Note 2: This should be covered by a home warranty—ask the seller.*

*Note: All gas furnaces and gas hot water heaters need a combustible exit to function (i.e., proper ventilation).* All nonelectric furnaces emit carbon monoxide, so all exhaust vents must be in accordance with uniform building codes.

*Note 3: Houses built prior to the mid-1960s may have asbestos as insulation wrap on heating ducts.* If in doubt, have it sampled and analyzed by a qualified professional.

If asbestos material is more than slightly damaged, or if you are going to make changes in the home that might disturb it, repair or removal by a professional is recommended. Before you have your house remodeled, find out whether asbestos materials are present.

_____If the hot water heater runs on gas, is the shutoff valve difficult to access?

_____If the hot water heater runs on gas, does it lack a vent to a perimeter wall? Gas furnaces emit harmful carbon monoxide.

_____Is the hot water heater tankless?

*Note : A tankless hot water heater allows for instant hot water. A tankless system does not store water and heat it over and over and over again. It heats the water when you turn on the tap, as it goes through the pipes.*

*Note 1: This should be covered by a home warranty—ask the seller.*

*Note 2: All gas furnaces and gas hot water heaters need a combustible exit to function (i.e., proper ventilation).* All nonelectric furnaces emit carbon monoxide, so all exhaust vents must be in accordance with uniform building codes.

_____If the hot water heater runs on gas, is the heater merely seated on the floor? A gas heater should be elevated from floor level.

*Note: Minimum height of elevation should be at least eighteen inches off the floor and properly strapped.*

_____Is there a pressure relief valve in the building?

_____Is there no containment for the pressure relief valve?

_____Is the hot water heater old? Find out the heater's age. The life expectancy of a hot water heater is approximately seven years.

*Replacement cost: $425–$900*

_____Does the hot water heater lack metal straps to secure it firmly in place?

*Note: Such straps are necessary to keep the hot water heater stable and secure during severe weather*

# Garage and Utility Room Notes

# Severe Weather Overview

Although your walk-through is now over, you should take a moment to recall what you've observed and formulate a coherent overview of one crucial aspect of the house—earthquake, tornado, hurricane, flooding, and lightning safety.

Depending upon what severe weather-prone area you may be living in, you need to ask the following questions:

Overall, how weather-safe is this house?

What needs to be done to make the house earthquake safe?

What needs to be done to make the house tornado safe?

What needs to be done to make the house hurricane safe?

What needs to be done to make the house lightning safe?

Here are some basic points to consider:

# Gas Shutoff

Make sure that tools for shutting off the gas main are readily accessible and that everyone knows where and how to shut off the gas. In the event of an earthquake, you should be able to turn off the gas quickly and easily. Gas shutoff kits are available online and at your local hardware/building supply store. Automatic shutoff devices are also available for installation for both propane tanks and direct connections.

**Propane Tanks**

Propane tanks may slide or topple during a significant earthquake, hurricane, or tornado. Both tank and pipes should be secure and shock resistant. We suggest the following:

1. The tank should be mounted on a continuous concrete pad and properly secured with mounting bolts.
2. Install a flexible hose connection; they are far less likely to fail during seismic shocks.

# House Grounding

If the house is in a lightning-prone area, you will want to ask if the house has a special grounding safe system installed in case of lightning strikes.
*Note: All houses are grounded; this is an additional grounding system.*

# Standing Items

No large, upright objects in the home—water heaters, wood stoves, built-in furnishings, and the like—should be left freestanding. They should be securely attached so as to not topple or move.

## Windows

Windows should be impact resistant or impact rated. This is especially crucial in living and sleeping areas. Again, an icon in the lower corner of the glass indicates that a window is impact resistant and thus severe weather safe.

*Note: Impact windows are more expensive than regular insulated windows.* Check to see if storm shutters are in place for all outside windows in areas prone to hurricanes, tornadoes, and lightning.

## Stairs, Landings, and Decks

Means of exit must be reliable and safe. Make sure that wooden stairs, landings, and decks are not wobbly or insecure and therefore prone to failure during severe weather.

## Garage Door

Check to see if the garage door has a pressure rating (tornado and hurricane).

## Roof

A gabled roof design is best in areas prone to hurricanes.

## Foundation

Make sure the foundation is not:
1. unreinforced; for reasons of safety and strength, concrete foundations should have steel rebar reinforcement;
2. severely cracked;
3. undermined at its perimeter.

# Basement Framing

In the basement:

1. points of contact between joists, beams, and posts should be reinforced with building-code-rated metal straps;
2. shear walls should be in place;
3. mud-sills should be bolted to the foundation.

*Note: If the house is deficient in the areas of foundation or basement framing, a seismic retrofit in earthquake, tornado, and hurricane-prone areas is called for.* Get estimates from licensed contractors in seismic/reinforcement retrofitting.

*We cannot underscore the importance of addressing these particular issues; the very survival of the home and the safety of your family may depend upon it.* This could also be a very expensive fix.

# Earthquakes, Tornadoes, Hurricanes, Flooding, and Lightning Safety

These are things that you won't be able to determine in your walk-through, and you need to ask these questions:

Is the home on or near an active earthquake fault zone?
Is the home around or near a frequent tornado area?
Is the home around or near a frequent hurricane area?
Is the home around or near a frequent flooding area?
Is the home around or near a frequent lightning area?

You will want to know this not only from a safety, precautionary, and preparedness standpoint, but from a resale value and insurance policy standpoint, as well.

This information may be obtained from the United States Geological Survey; a variety of state, federal, and county publications or offices; the Internet; neighbors; or from the county geologist (if available).

# Severe Weather Overview Notes

# The Walk-Through Worksheet

## The Front of the House

|  | House One | House Two | House Three |
|---|---|---|---|
| Landscaping | | | |
| Driveway | | | |
| Front Walkway | | | |
| Destructive Root Systems | | | |
| Stairs and Landings | | | |
| Concrete or Brick | | | |
| Porch and Overhang | | | |
| Siding | | | |
| Paint or Stain | | | |
| Front Door | | | |
| Garage Door | | | |
| Sills and Trim | | | |
| Windows | | | |
| Utilities | | | |

**Totals**

**Notes**

## The Back of the House

| | House One | House Two | House Three |
|---|---|---|---|
| Fences and Walls | | | |
| Patio | | | |
| Deck | | | |
| Patio Door | | | |
| Exterior Lighting | | | |
| Sills and Trim | | | |
| Windows | | | |
| Retaining Wal | | | |
| Landscaping | | | |
| Jacuzzi and Swimming Pool | | | |
| Sewage | | | |

**Totals**

**Notes**

**Roof and Foundation**

| | House One | House Two | House Three |
|---|---|---|---|
| Roof | | | |
| Asphalt Composite Shingle | | | |
| Wood Shake | | | |
| Tar and Gravel | | | |
| Slate and Concrete Tiles | | | |
| Roof Line | | | |
| Fireplace and Chimney | | | |
| Gutters and Downspouts | | | |
| Flashing | | | |
| Foundation | | | |

**Totals**

**Notes**

## Interior of the House

|  | House One | House Two | House Three |
|---|---|---|---|
| Front Hall and Foyer | | | |
| Floor | | | |
| Heating | | | |
| Leaks | | | |
| Lighting | | | |
| Coat Closet | | | |
| Safety | | | |
| Wall Surfaces | | | |
| Look Out for Skylights | | | |
| **Totals** | | | |

**Notes**

# LIVING ROOM

|  | House One | House Two | House Three |
|---|---|---|---|
| Door | | | |
| Electrical | | | |
| Fireplace | | | |
| Floor | | | |
| Heating | | | |
| Leaks | | | |
| Lighting | | | |
| Windows | | | |
| Furnishings | | | |
| Wall Surfaces | | | |
| **Totals** | | | |

**Notes**

## Dining Room

| | House One | House Two | House Three |
|---|---|---|---|
| Electrical | | | |
| Floor | | | |
| Heating | | | |
| Leaks | | | |
| Lighting | | | |
| Windows | | | |
| Wall Surfaces | | | |
| Thermostat | | | |

**Totals**

**Notes**

## Kitchen

|  | House One | House Two | House Three |
|---|---|---|---|
| Appliances | | | |
| Cabinets | | | |
| Countertops | | | |
| Electrical | | | |
| Faucet and Sink | | | |
| Floor | | | |
| Leaks | | | |
| Lighting | | | |
| Pantry | | | |
| Plumbing | | | |
| Windows | | | |
| Wall Surfaces | | | |
| **Totals** | | | |

**Notes**

**Family Room and Breakfast Nook**

| | House One | House Two | House Three |
|---|---|---|---|
| Electrical | | | |
| Floor | | | |
| Heating | | | |
| Leaks | | | |
| Lighting | | | |
| Windows | | | |
| Wall Surfaces | | | |

**Totals**

**Notes**

## Laundry Room

|  | House One | House Two | House Three |
|---|---|---|---|
| Appliances |  |  |  |
| Door |  |  |  |
| Electrical |  |  |  |
| Floor |  |  |  |
| Plumbing |  |  |  |
| Windows |  |  |  |
| Wall Surfaces |  |  |  |
| **Totals** |  |  |  |

**Notes**

## Bedrooms

| | House One | House Two | House Three |
|---|---|---|---|
| Closets | | | |
| Doors | | | |
| Electrical | | | |
| Floor | | | |
| Heating | | | |
| Leaks | | | |
| Lighting | | | |
| Windows | | | |
| Wall Surfaces | | | |

## Totals

## Notes

## Bathrooms

| | House One | House Two | House Three |
|---|---|---|---|
| Ceiling | | | |
| Door | | | |
| Electrical | | | |
| Faucet and Sink | | | |
| Floors and Walls | | | |
| Heating | | | |
| Lighting | | | |
| Shower and Bath | | | |
| Additional Trouble | | | |
| Toilet | | | |

## Totals

## Notes

## Basement

| | House One | House Two | House Three |
|---|---|---|---|
| Doors | | | |
| Earthquake Safety | | | |
| Foundation | | | |
| Framing | | | |
| Lighting | | | |
| Staircase | | | |
| Water Woes | | | |
| **Totals** | | | |

**Notes**

## Garage and Utility Room

| | House One | House Two | House Three |
|---|---|---|---|
| Garage | | | |
| Cars | | | |
| Door | | | |
| Electrical Outlets | | | |
| Foundation | | | |
| Lighting | | | |
| **Totals** | | | |

**Notes**

## Utility Room

| | House One | House Two | House Three |
|---|---|---|---|
| Furnace | | | |
| Air-Conditioning Unit | | | |
| Hot Water Heater | | | |

## Totals

## Notes

# Severe Weather Questions

| | House One | House Two | House Three |
|---|---|---|---|
| Gas | | | |
| Standing Items | | | |
| Windows | | | |
| Doors | | | |
| Stairs and Landings | | | |
| Decks | | | |
| Foundation | | | |
| Basement Framing | | | |
| Seismic Retrofitting | | | |
| **Totals** | | | |

**Notes**

# At a Glance

**House One**

Address: _____

Agent Info: _____
Date: _____

**Asking Price:** _____

**Worksheet Total:** _____

**Difference from Asking Price:** _____

**Notes**

**House Two**

Address: _____

Agent Info: _____
Date: _____

**Asking Price:** _____


**Worksheet Total:** _____

**Difference from Asking Price:** _____

**Notes**

## House Three

Address: _____

Agent Info: _____

Date: _____

**Asking Price:** _____

**Worksheet Total:** _____

**Difference from Asking Price:** _____

**Notes**

## House One Info/Offer

**Address:** _____

**Agent:** _____

**Date:** _____

**Asking Price:** _____

**Worksheet Total:** _____

**Difference from Asking:** _____

**Offer Price:** _____

**House Two Info/Offer**

Address: _____

Agent: _____

Date: _____

Asking Price: _____

Worksheet Total: _____   _____

Difference from Asking: _____

Offer Price: _____

## House Three Info/Offer

**Address:** _____

**Agent:** _____

**Date:** _____

**Asking Price:** _____

**Worksheet Total:** _____

**Difference from Asking:** _____

**Offer Price:** _____

**More Notes**